T0339356

No One Will Know You Tomorrow

NAJWAN DARWISH

No One Will Know You Tomorrow

SELECTED POEMS, 2014–2024

Translated from the Arabic by
Kareem James Abu-Zeid

A MARGELLOS
WORLD REPUBLIC OF LETTERS BOOK

Yale UNIVERSITY PRESS | NEW HAVEN & LONDON

The Margellos World Republic of Letters is dedicated to making literary works from around the globe available in English through translation. It brings to the English-speaking world the work of leading poets, novelists, essayists, philosophers, and playwrights from Europe, Latin America, Africa, Asia, and the Middle East to stimulate international discourse and creative exchange.

Contents

From *Exhausted on the Cross* 135

"A Breeze from Üsküdar" and Other Poems *151*

From *Weary of Walking in the Barzakh* *169*

No One Will Know You Tomorrow

Translator's Introduction

Born in Jerusalem in 1978, Najwan Darwish has emerged, over the past few decades, as one of the most unique and powerful voices not only of contemporary Palestinian poetry, but of Arabic-language poetry as a whole. Although his work is deeply rooted in the geography of Palestine, it is also remarkably expansive, moving almost effortlessly through a range of landscapes and histories. It is this expansiveness, this cultural, linguistic, and historical openness, that is undoubtedly one of the most salient reasons that readers from all over the world have been drawn to Darwish's poetry; at the time of this writing, his work has been translated into more than thirty languages and counting. A dual movement—simultaneously through both space and time—characterizes much of the poetry of the present collection, which comprises a selection from the past decade of Darwish's work.

Before exploring the broader expanse of the many landscapes Darwish visits, let us start with the one place that crops up the most frequently, and the most poignantly, in his recent work: Haifa. Darwish has split his time between Haifa and Jerusalem for several decades. Jerusalem made more frequent appearances in his earlier poetry, more often than not as a kind of cruel and torturing goddess, and even, at one moment, as "the older sister of Sodom and Go-morrah." This characterization contrasts sharply with that of Haifa, which, located as it is between the verdant pine-covered mountain Carmel and the endless blue of the Med-iterranean Sea, appears time and again in this volume as a kind of multifaceted Paradise. Even the title of the slim po-etry collection from which the opening poems of this book are drawn, *A Chair on the Walls of Acre,* is a subtle reference to Haifa, for those ancient walls are in fact sea walls. Those who have been to Acre (also known as Akka or Akko) know that the city of Haifa can be clearly seen across the water—it's less than fifteen miles from Acre to Haifa, as the crow flies. Furthermore, on clear days Darwish can see the city of Acre from the windows of his apartment in Haifa.

This poetry evokes, both explicitly and implicitly, the rich and varied history of Haifa across the millennia, a history of conquest and counter-conquest, rife with a multitude of civi-lizations and invasions (Canaanite, Egyptian, Persian, Greek, Roman, Byzantine, Islamic, Mongol, and Crusader, to name only a few). Although this poetry embodies a remarkably open-ended and non-exclusionary view of identity, it pulls no punches when it comes to the more modern colonial projects of the French and the British, as well as the current Occupation. Until the Nakba in 1948, Haifa was (in varying degrees at different points of time) a vibrant and thriving Pal-estinian city, home to Muslims, Christians, and Jews, in addi-tion to pilgrims of other faiths. But following the Nakba, well over 90 percent of the city's Palestinian population was ex-pelled, and their homes were confiscated. Najwan Darwish's relationship to Haifa is thus a complex and open-ended one. "What are you?" he asks in the poem "A Morning Note for the Paradise of Carmel," before continuing: "The ghost of a dead lover? / A garden that abandonment bought / before locking its door?" Later in the same poem, Darwish mourns the paradox of being a so-called exile within his own ancestral homeland.

Perhaps one of the poet's more radical acts is to stubbornly see Haifa through the eyes of the natural world on the one hand (the limitless potential and vast freedom of the Mediterranean Sea, as well as the green of Mount Carmel's pines, which can never be colonized), and through the city's vast history on the other, an expanse of millennia that reduces the present political moment to a mere speck of dust. Nowhere do we see this historical gaze more clearly than in the poem "Mount Carmel," which evokes the specificity of many of Haifa's historically Arab neighborhoods (Wadi Nisnas, Wadi Salib, Kababir) while simultaneously delving into the history and cultural pluralism that make this city so unique:

> Sometimes the church bells reach me
> from the depths of Wadi Nisnas;
> and some mornings the call to prayer
> comes in quietly from the Istiqlal Mosque (borne
> on an ancient breeze from Wadi Salib);
> and the Baha'is keep giving alms
> and filling the city with Persian gardens
> that escaped from Shiraz;
> and in Kababir
> the followers of Mirza Ghulam Ahmad
> maintain their naps of devotion
> and hunt for Truth in the Prophet's words;
> as for the holy men among the Druze,
> their poems reach me from the temple

at the foot of Mount Hermon
like the white headscarves of their women
(the ones that hide a thousand years of darkness).

Yet this is not "activist" poetry in any usual sense of the word. "I don't think of my poetry as activism," Darwish recently asserted in an interview in *The Guardian*. "I do that outside of it. Poetry is like praying. You can't do activism inside a prayer. It's more of a spiritual practice." Indeed, in poems such as these, it also feels as if Darwish is looking at the land through the eyes of eternity, though it is an eternity that is not without wounding and mortality. There is Paradise in the land, yes, and eternity, but it is always a Paradise lost, a kind of mortal and evanescent eternity. As the acclaimed Chilean poet Raúl Zurita has so poignantly written: "Najwan Darwish's poetry travels through the villages, landscapes, neighborhoods, cities, and towns of a history that is three millennia old, one that, in each of its corners, preserves the remains of a permanently shattered eternity, as if there were an underlying god, not named, who took pleasure in weaving together suffering and misfortune."

It often feels that the poet is shackled to the divine, bound up with some contradictory God who doles out blessings and grace with one hand, while inflicting no end of tragedy and suffering with the other. As such, the poet admonishes God, time and again, for the loss and abandonment experienced to some degree by all the living, but which is amplified and exaggerated in the condition of those who were born as Palestinians. And we readers are required, time and again, to bear witness to these spiritual addresses. This is particularly apparent in the selection from Darwish's collection *Discourses* (*Mukhāṭabāt*), the title of which is a reference to the tenth-century Sufi mystic Al-Niffari's own *Dis-*

courses. The latter are evocative spiritual texts that give voice to experiences of unity with God. Each of these begins with the words "He said to me," where the "He" refers to God, or perhaps the higher Self of the author. Najwan Darwish reworks this genre, creating a very different kind of spiritual discourse, one shot through with loss and destruction, yet never utterly devoid of glory and joy:

> He said to me:
> I cleaved my life in two
> and further cleaved the halves,
> to say nothing of the cleavings wrought
> by invaders and tyrants,
> by despair, and hope, and urban devastation.
> I've only ever seen my life in tatters,
> fractured like clouds,
> though from time to time it pulls itself together
> to rain down—
> that's why, no matter where I'm exiled,
> there will be flowers
> and verdant fields.

Loss, abandonment, destruction, devasation: These motifs are ubiquitous in this collection. The loss at stake is more than merely the loss of land (though that too is ubiquitous). The loss is also one of plurality and diversity, as we see in the collection *You Are Not a Poet in Granada.* It should be noted that Muslim Andalusia (i.e., Al-Andalus), and the city of Granada in particular, occupy a prominent place in the Arab imaginary—they connote a kind of Golden Age of thought and culture, an emblem of openness, tolerance, and mutual respect. This was no monolithic culture, but a place where many faiths and cultures came together, where difference was respected rather than feared. But these hopes and dreams were shattered with the fall of Granada—the last Muslim stronghold in Al-Andalus—into the hands of the Catholic monarchs Isabella and Ferdinand II in 1492. "These are the keys to Paradise," the Muslim emir Muhammad XII is reputed to have said as he handed over the keys of the city. This transfer of power would soon lead to the forced expulsion or conversion of the city's Muslim and Jewish residents. At moments, Granada parallels Haifa, and Al-Andalus all of Palestine, in representing a kind of Paradise lost, as we see in the poem "I Don't Claim" (though it should be noted that Darwish's evocations of Granada and Al-Andalus are far too complex and open-ended to be pinned down in any definitive way):

> My country is an Andalus of poems and water
> that I lost
> and am still losing—
> in loss
> it becomes my country.

The precarious nature of Palestinian existence has come to the fore in an almost unbearable manner in recent months, in the aftermath of October 7th. Today as I write this—in early 2024—no fewer than 30,000 Palestinians have been killed in Gaza, the majority of them women and children, in addition to more than 70,000 Palestinians who have been wounded. These are numbers that defy the imagination, defy our own humanity. And tomorrow the numbers will be greater still. In many ways, the present "conflict"—far too small a word for the ongoing carnage and the displacement of an entire population—is what Palestinians have been enduring since 1948, though currently with a far greater intensity and ferocity than in the past. Darwish's poetry—at once anti-nationalist yet profoundly and personally invested in the Palestinian cause—is a necessary intervention in this polarized situation, an indictment of the brutality and injustices that Palestinians are facing. It is a relentless bearing witness: to history, to the land, to violence, yet without ever falling into the facile trap of victimhood; all the while retaining a sense of power, dignity, and compassion. There is a deep moral and spiritual imperative here, an inability to turn away from the voices of the past and the present, an impulse to allow the voices of the dead (so many dead) to rise up through the poet and speak again, in the present moment:

> I return
> because one must return,
> because the dead must rise again.

And at the same time, human frailty is ever present— moments of weakness, hesitation, and fear. Moments when it seems that being Palestinian, being subject to such degradation, death, and humiliation on a daily basis, is simply too much. In the poem "Not This Cup," Darwish gives voice to such human frailty by evoking the words of another, more famous figure from Palestine, someone whose compassion and forgiveness have become proverbial, despite his own frailties and moments of weakness:

> Lord, I'll swallow it, any cup you want—
> just not my country's cup.

In addition to Christ, a host of other literary and historical figures from the Middle East make both subtle and prominent appearances in this book, for Darwish is nothing if not a student of history, and of the Arabic literary tradition (to say nothing of the many other literary traditions from different regions of the world that he has immersed himself in). From some of the most prominent pre-Islamic poets to the Prophet Muhammad himself and the pagan Quraysh who opposed him, from medieval Arab poets and theologians to modern writers and singers—all these voices find their way into Darwish's work. It is not so much a matter of taking sides with certain figures over others, or of espousing certain worldviews over others, but rather of mining the wisdom of each of these figures, as well as considering their varied roles in history, and allowing all of this to be born anew in a brilliant reworking of tradition—a reworking that is part and parcel of the tradition itself.

In this sweeping collection, there is no glory that is not touched by loss, no loss that is not touched by sacredness and glory; no immortality that is not touched by death, no eternity that is not touched by time. Death is a presence that is always lurking in the background, or bursting into the foreground. This is at once the human condition and, much more acutely, the Palestinian condition in this day and age. Najwan Darwish's unforgettable verse gives voice to all of this, and draws us in with its irresistible humanity.

From *A Chair on the Walls of Acre*

THE WAVES OF ACRE

What's cleansed by the waves
with all this foam?
The invisible raiment of the gods?

It's hard to believe that all this ceaseless motion
is merely for washing the feet
of these aging stones
or for dallying with the sands of the shore.

I've heard, of course, of the tides,
the ebb and flow,
but in moments like these
I cannot trust the laws of physics.

All I can do is think
like a man wounded by existence,
and all I can hope for
is to be
like the raiment of the gods—
perhaps one day the waves will come
and wash me clean.

WHAT MORE COULD I WANT?

What more could I want from the Lord?
He's already given me
a village on the sea,
and he's favored me
with the inkling of a breeze from the mountain.

It's true the invaders' banners
are like specks of dirt in the eyes,
but I'm one of those who stayed in the village,
and I'm thinking of the ones
who were expelled from it.

I close my eyes,
I close them often:
No speck can touch this beauty.

TAL AL-SAMAK[1]

Come to Tal al-Samak.
The waves have their words, audible,
and the ruins of the old harbor
will wake the openings
of all the pre-Islamic poems
from their long slumber:
Have the Haifans
left anything unsaid? . . .
She told us she would soon be parting . . .
The abodes are desolate . . .
Emptied of its people . . .

Just come, come to Tal al-Samak.

IN NATURE'S CELL

Where can a man go
to escape the face of death?
Death is the sea, the mountain, the breeze,
it blooms in fragments of love
and is crowned in every wedding the seasons tend.

Where can death go
to escape the face of man?
Man is the sea, the mountain, the breeze,
he blooms in fragments of love
and is crowned in every wedding the seasons tend.

In nature's prison cell
they find themselves neighbors, are forced
to become fast friends:
death, and man.

CITIZENS OF DUST

You wake in grace,
in what the Creator, ever bountiful,
was freely granting,
the One who bestows love
and joy.

It's time to wake in grace—
you who have always stood up to misery,
like crowds rising against their executioner.

The earth—all of it—is a house of refuge.
The people—all of them—are citizens of dust.

EMBRACE

I was confused and wet,
and my arms were torn as they tried to embrace
the mountains, the valleys, the plains,
while the sea I loved pulled me under
time and again,
until what was once a lover's body
became a corpse
floating on the surface.

Confused and wet, my corpse
stretches out its arms now
(like my living body once did),
desperate
for the embrace of the sea
that keeps pulling it under.

A MERE MORTAL

"Who am I?" I asked my self,
but it paid no heed
to the ramblings of a mere mortal—
eternity is its solitary confinement,
immortality alone concerns it.

VILLAGERS REFLECTING ON JOY

Must we be emperors
to seize the moment by its wrist
and drag it to a high and shaded balcony?
Must we become emperors
to dare to pluck a rose
from your garden, God?

A VERSE BY HAFEZ IBRAHIM
ON THE SHORE OF HAIFA

Like a kid in third grade whose teacher was murdered,
I walked in the darkness,
abandoned on the shore after midnight,
crying out:
"I'm the sea, and the pearls are hidden within me.
Did they ask the divers about my shells?"[2]
I kept shouting it,
waiting for the gods to hear me:
"I'm the sea,
and the pearls are hidden within me."
My teacher was murdered
and I'll keep reciting that verse, hopelessly,
until the gods hear me
and reply.
I'm not sad
and I'm not afraid
and I don't care
that I've been abandoned on a dark shore.
"I'm the sea, and the pearls
are hidden within me."
Do the shells feel pride?
Do the fish remember
the ships' melodies?
And what sea is this
coming at me
dressed like a trusted adviser:
"They'll arrest you if you keep screaming in Arabic.
They'll open fire.
Stop it, please: I'm tired of your blood
spilling on my shore."

Who would I be if I stopped?
I'll keep on—
even if the gods hear me,
even if they reply.

WORDS FOR WADI SALIB[3]

You couldn't believe how I'd grown
and I couldn't believe
how you'd been abandoned.

Who'd believe their own hands and face
had turned into ruins
to be bought and sold?

Valley of the shadow of death
and of life's shadow, too,
our shadows are breaking and gathering
on the balconies of your homes,
and we'll keep at it: coming together
and saying farewell
like two waves lost in our great sea.

NOT THIS CUP

I

This tower that refuses to go down
though all the bulldozers of the world
strike at its foundation;
this icon that keeps gleaming,
up there on the wall,
despite the slinging of the mud,
despite the lowliness that clings
to its lowly brother;
this love that refuses to end
though there's no one left
to claim it now.

Lord, I'll swallow it, any cup you want—
just not my country's cup.

II

Lord, all things are growing old,
and only misery
restores its youth.
Lord, all things are dying
but tragedy:
it keeps being reborn, a virgin,
from the foam of this lost sea.
Lord, all things are crumbling
except this grief: its two murdered fists
are breaking down my door.

TORMENTED BY JOY

When a table of manna and solace comes down to you,
and pitchers filled with the wines of the gods,
the likes of which you've never seen,
and you find yourself alone there,
standing like a eulogizer at the head of the table,
your feelings, now, are like my own,
here in joy's solitary confinement.
Yes, I have a sea, and a mountain too—
but exile has taken
everyone I love.

DAYS OF HELL

While we were in hell
we couldn't say
that we were in hell,
and that was the worst of it.

To this very moment
it still seems so absurd—
our belated confession.

WAITING

Write your orphaned line.
Take a step and enter
the month of August.
Cross the years and lay yourself
in the makeshift grave of time.
Your ancestors are there, all of them—
they're lying in the dirt,
they're waiting for you to join them.

BALAD AL-SHAYKH[4]

I've been to Balad al-Shaykh
to greet the ones resting there.
I stood in the dark and recited the Fatiha.

Lord, even here,
in this graveyard—
must I stand alone?

A RIDING SONG WITH BADAWI AL-JABAL 5

I have inexhaustible stores of compassion
that I lavish on all the wretched and oppressed
—Badawi al-Jabal

I lavished them on the demonstrators
forcing their way into the square
like white sails in the midday blue,
I lavished them on the ones who wake at dawn,
the ones who sleep in prison,
I lavished them on their estrangement,
their hollowed-out history,
their hijacked days,
the papers they buried in my chest
after splitting it open,
I lavished them on the truncated paths,
the confiscated water,
the stolen land.
I lavished them on the gleam of glasses in empty palaces.
(How could I raise a toast
after their glasses had been shattered?)
I lavished them on the quivering earth
in divans whose authors do not die.
I stood on the road and cried out:
Lavish the pain of the pre-Islamic peoples
and the weddings of faith illumined
by chandeliers of sorrow
hanging from the Kingdom.
I cried out: Lavish this love
piled up by grandmothers more ancient than trees.
And it was as if I were a ghost

that didn't know it was a ghost
and I was screaming: Lavish it all.
Yet all of Korah's wealth
weighed me down,
and Solomon's many purported treasures,
and all the misfortunes of the Arabs. . . .

In the middle of the road
I cry out
while the passersby avert their eyes
and hurry on their way.

YOU SAID

You said you'd feed the people
with a handful of wheat
from your small threshing floor,
from the opening of a song,
from the light
that's setting in your eyes.
You said you'd do this
despite abandonment's burden.

And all I could do was believe you
as you broke your body into pieces
for this pilgrimage of strange birds. . . .

Here you are now,
a handful of wheat for the people.

THE HELL OF MY PEOPLE

You can't say anything about my people that I don't
   already know.
Just as I came down from their sky, their clouds,
   their mountains,
I also experienced their dark valleys and caves,
and I have a complete copy
of the book of their sins;
and even their hyenas and snakes—
I feel for them and love them.

Doubts about my god hurled me around,
but I never once doubted my people.
To them I attributed
all that's worthy of life,
and my love for them is not
the only thing that's blind—
I too am blind,
and I've surrendered the reins to them,
though I know they're leading me to hell.

IN THE BEGINNING

I remember you in abandonment.
I lose you to exile in the morning and late afternoon,
I lose you to exile in the evenings of invisible people,
I lose you to exile and forget you,
a country that sent itself into exile,
a country
that's abandonment itself.

In the beginning was not the Word.
In the beginning
was Abandonment alone.

IN ABANDONMENT

I told the woman who shares my destiny:
You're like myself, compelled
to be lost.
I told her: Love and walls can crack
in an instant,
and you and I will stand naked before time,
naked as the summer with all its stickiness,
naked as the winter with all its trembling.
But where did you put my destiny
(which is your own),
the one I looked for this morning
but could not find?
I trusted you with it,
that trifle we keep for memory's sake.
Did you squander it
like the moneyed women do?
Or did you trade it for household goods?
Was it good for anything at all?
Should I mourn its loss?
It's true I no longer feel a thing
in the darkness of this deserted house,
but it *was* my destiny, after all,
and here you are, silent
in the face of its loss.

You're from a lost country, she said,
a lost planet, and I lived with you
in an abandoned land,
an abandoned house,
and we drank from two abandoned glasses.

Your books were wasted and abandoned,
and all we were waiting for was abandonment
to fall upon us with the setting sun. . . .
This is your habit, she said,
amidst abandonment's disruptions.

Then her words blended into mine,
and I couldn't tell which of us
flew into a rage
and told the other:
Don't be rude, now—
we're guests of abandonment, after all.

IN OBLIVION

A memorial for the dead?
What about forgetting them completely,
utterly, forever?

Even that's not possible,
for they inhabit the absolute—the rock
of oblivion.

FATE

Bring the book of my fate,
the one I keep losing,
the one you keep finding.

Bring it just once
and help me tear it up
and burn it
and scatter the ashes.

There's no other way to free our fate
from the confines of its pages.

HARDLY BREATHE

The grief overflows from the rooms
every time I, like some ghost,
enter your abandoned homes, my hand
clinging to my end.
I fall asleep with my ruin
and I wake with it.
It's lonely, becoming so familiar
with solitude
and walking so far on its path.
How heavy is the abandonment that fills your homes?
How heavy *are* the abandoned homes?
I enter their hollow hearts, and can hardly breathe.
No Arabs
or Persians
or Byzantines
know me now.
Didn't I have a history?
And how did I lose, on the way, poems
that were the world itself,
the world unfurling in an instant?
And how were *you* lost?
How did you take my share of loss
and leave abandonment in its stead, a planet
without a ribcage?
You left it to me, in my keeping,
and if I said I was leaving
there'd be no one here at all—
no one but abandonment,
with its throaty voice
that's swallowing my own.

QUIETLY RETURNING

Why did the gods abandon her?
Out of love
or impotence?

Sometimes I imagine that small goddesses
are quietly returning
(they're resting now in a thicket of reeds
or under a linden tree)
and that I'm like them:
I too am quietly returning
to the land I abandoned.

I NEVER KNEW

I never knew anyone
more particular than you:
All the languages were sleeping
with poets and warriors and kings,
but *you* accepted nothing less
than God's own bed.

I never knew anyone
happier than you:
The screams rise from hell
in all the tongues,
but you alone are the language
of the people of Paradise.

I never knew anyone
more miserable than myself
here in the lowest circle of hell,
but still I don't cry out—
I wouldn't want
to put you on the spot.

A NOTEBOOK

You lose it for two days,
and your life's lost with it.
And when you stumble upon it,
you find your life again,
light
and delicate:
No thief ever comes this way
without asking for it.

AN OTTOMAN TUNE
(Jerusalem, 1914)

They're awake in the village's dawn
to bid farewell to the boy
heading off in the Seferberlik.[6]

The morning star
was a betrayal of trust.
No dawn would ever
bring that child back.

NEAR THE SHRINE OF SAINT NAUM[7]

I stood in the red church,
its tiny domes like buds
blossoming in stone,
I stood near the saint's resting place
while a tourist laid her cheek on the tombstone
to hear his beating heart.
But I was no tourist,
and the saint left the room with me,
and the church the builders wrote in his memory
was nothing more
than a passing dream in his eternal sleep.

The tourists come in vain,
as do the believers.

THE PIANO PLAYER'S STROKES

No one can pen the piano player's strokes on the old radio,
there on the kitchen table I stumbled upon in Wadi Salib, in
that apartment I stumbled upon in Haifa—Haifa, which the
Creator stumbled upon in one of His mornings of splendor.

No one will understand the mornings of my mournful
splendor, or how my despair drips with joy, or how quickly
my mood turns when I hear the Zionist news on the old
radio—which, from that moment forward, no longer
concerns me in the slightest.

LOST

That which is lost for forever,
that which that no one knows
but me—
I want you to know it too.
If it's lost but you know it
it's as if
it was never lost.

My hands are open,
and in every home I pour it out—
the childhood
I once had.

OBRIGADO[8]

Don't thank anyone—
you're overdoing it, this obrigado.
God alone should be thanked for calamities,
and these people are no gods. . . .

From what prolific wells,
from what clouds
are you gurgling out this obrigado?

How can I incite you to rage, good peoples?
Rage is love's dignity,
and satisfaction's a steed—the colonizers and exploiters,
the stealers of dreams,
jump onto its back.
If someone must be thanked for these calamities,
then let's thank rage:
Obrigado, rage.
Obrigado.

IN PRAISE OF EXPERIENCE

My child, there are words you'll understand
only with experience.
I, for one, learned only with experience
things I hadn't learned
from a whole lifetime.
Imagine this: The birds I'd heard chirping in my cell
—I had no idea where they came from—
were nothing but pangs of hunger in my belly.
It was thanks to them that I restored my ties
with the trees and the sky, and with our good language,
which turns hunger into a poignant bird
of faint and intermittent singing.

A SUN OUTSIDE OF TRAGEDY

I said I'd bask in a sun
outside of tragedy,
so I put out a chair of straw
and sat down.
I said I'd bask in the love that was stored
for years, before misery set in—
as if creation had just begun,
as if mines and shrapnel
hadn't torn my face, my memory,
time and again,
until I *had* no face
but these looted, bulldozed hills
(these hills shot through with walls),
until I had no memory
but this forgetful,
lying,
lifeless
sky.

There's no sun today,
no sun outside of tragedy.

Light cannot be held,
neither can time.
Even noise
cannot be grasped.
The most you can do
is hold your head in your hands
until all light, time, and noise
fade away.

A sentence in the swelter of contemplation:
Nothing tortures quite like joy.
Joy's left us to our thoughts now,
and to the torment that goes with them.

May God give water
to our ancient miseries.

Mountains crumble in my head,
and rain-drenched meadows slip away, one
after the other.
Even the sky,
the single sky above all people,
is no longer mine.

I want these words to take me back thirty years,
before the trees were cut down, the valleys bulldozed,
when the olives were still there,
and the pomegranates,
and, perhaps, a future veiled by the past's kaffiyeh.

A country that moves like a gondola
between nightmare and dream.

Can these invaders really steal it—
the past that was once the future?

The paper kite
slipped from my hands,
as did the longings,
the love and the hate,
and even the land.
But I'm neither regretful
nor afraid—

regret and fear
also slipped away.

THE POEM OF RETURNING HOME

I wandered through every delight,
but now memory's unable
to bring back those palaces I visited
or fled from as they clutched at my robes.

Only this aging apartment,
forgotten like a wound on Carmel's neck,[9]
managed to be my home.

LIFE REVIEW AT THIRTY-SEVEN

Ten years were taken from me:
women passing through,
false friends,
relatives of the nth degree,
the filth of the occupation,
the misery of unfulfilled love,
books,
rooms and travels,
the inklings of dreams and delusions.

I'm casting them away now, without hesitation,
to return to twenty-seven
and foolishly storm them once more—
all my dubious prospects.

AS FOR MY SINGING

"Sing, sing before we slit your throat."
Did they think fear
would disturb my song?
True, I was scared of life,
but death
is the last thing I'm afraid of.
Why would a free man fear
to meet a friend?

So let our embrace be tinged with blood.
As for my singing in this moment,
I want it to be perfect.

My freedom lies in this:
No matter what they do,
the murderers still
cannot disturb my song.

From *With Every Storm That Comes: A Season in London*

A DINNER INVITATION

I told myself: If you want to see her now,
look where the sky meets the mountain
as it descends to the sea.

Her invitation's eternal now,
and her home is time.

So let others sing their lamentations,
let them surrender to separation.
I'll sing nothing but your promise,
nothing but your life, falling
like a late spring rain,
your life like a summer breeze.

Let others sing their sorrow.
I'll sing your joy—
not even death could break it.

WHILE YOU'RE WAITING AT THE END

I

I told her: Write anywhere, anytime.
You're consummating defeat
yet they're calling you a victor.
Write, for you'll gain nothing
but your losses.
Write, for you'll lose nothing
but what you've written.
Write, and lose.
Show them how loss can be,
show them how palaces are built, and destroyed.
And sigh, sigh like a queen
on your throne of endless losses.

I I

I told her:
Now you're empty of all hope,
so write your emptiness, your freedom
from suspicion and misgivings,
and take a look around you:
You can't distinguish the heavens
from the shrines of everlasting rest.

Passers-by in history
erase other passers-by.

III

I told her: Write while you're waiting at the end,
write while they deliver you to death,
write on death's threshold,
and write while you, indifferent,
look into death's eyes.
Believer, write it:
Heresy conquers all.
Heretic, write it:
Belief is all there is.

ON THE WAY TO TIPAZA[10]

If I could,
I'd put eternity on the breakfast table for you,
I'd tighten my grip on time
so it showed you only its delights.

But I can't,
and therein lies my tragedy.

RECALLING A TRYST IN A PARK

And who am I in the halls,
who in the mills?
All around us the lilies were crushed,
all around us was the earth,
and all around us follies were blooming.
"This is the way of lovely women—
they're given to deception,"
as the song goes.[11]
Then we laughed
and I didn't blame you.

And after all these years, still
I do not blame you.

YOU THINK OF A HOUSE

At the bus stop in the morning
you think of a house in a town by the sea,
you claim it's the mother of all the cities of the world.
You think of that small house
as you walk in the funeral of the pulsing free market,
in the last rites where every step is sold
by the square inch.

At the bus stop in the morning
you say life's running late
or that you've missed life's bus,
but still you stand there, thinking
of a small house hidden by the breeze
and exposed by the pines at the foot of Mount Carmel.

WITH EVERY STORM THAT COMES

I remember you in the storm
because you *are* the storm.
It was only through stubbornness
that we managed to live in you.
If I let go of my hands this morning
will I lose you forever?
Will I fall into chasms of loss,
chasms that multiply,
chasms whose cold laughter you hear
as you leave all hope behind?

If I let go of my hands this morning
will I lose myself forever—
the self I lost yesterday,
the self I'll lose tomorrow?
Fate brings it back
only so I can lose it again.
How will the people understand
that it was through stubbornness that we lived,
caught
between being uprooted
and holding our ground?
And how will *I* understand
why, with every storm that comes,
I'm reminded of my home?

A WAVE OF PEOPLE

A wave of people breaks against you,
a wave
of tangled fears,
migrations, guilt.
It's all the same
if it crests in abundance
or crashes
on scarcity's shores.
And it's all the same
if it breaks itself against you
or pulls you under.
Believe that you are the spray
falling on the sea
and you will be at peace.

It's all the same
if it breaks itself against you
or pulls you under.

JUST LIKE THEM

I won't hide from you
that my heart is there
against justice,
against the law I see only as a prison cell,
where truth is forced to kneel
on nights that have no dawn,
on mornings that no night follows.

I heard you tonight singing to rebels,
I heard the secrets in your voice
and said to myself:
You're a rebel just like them,
and your passions hurl you around
like nights that have no dawn,
like dawns that no night follows,
like death, which is only the beginning.
So be where they are,
be the tempests that defy the sea—
defeated, yet you resist,
victorious because of that resistance.
Be in those tempests.
Stand against justice—justice
is what you are.

MERCILESSLY

Let's look at this thicket,
let's widen this breach in the heart,
a breach whose branches lengthen
and burst into leaf,
a breach in which a history was lost
and is still being lost
with the same cruelty.
In the breach, loss
keeps on expanding
to devour the nightmares and the dreams,
the newborn's songs
and the dead man's farewell,
to devour even love,
to devour the people stashing it away
in the tears of reunion,
in the handkerchiefs they're waving.
A breach that expands and contracts,
a breach,
a breach.
Better we hold it at bay
and silence the news of its savage branches.
Better we bless these branches
as they grow, mercilessly.

A breach,
a breach.

I HAD A WORD

I had some words
for that anguished woman,
heedless of herself,
sunk in what she thought was joy—
she couldn't tell her lover from her victim.
I had some words
for that woman, heroic
in her cowardice,
that suicide
who paid no heed to any god.
I'd see her at dawn, her hair a mess;
and I'd see her in the depths of night, her eyes
polished with kohl
and wine
and sacred verses.
Always I swallowed my words—
so often
that I no longer had anything left to say,
or so I thought.

I had a word and lost it,
or so I thought.

BLINK OF AN EYE

You return from a workday as long as the blink of an eye,
a flickering eye,
a flickering heart in the midday heat,
in the snow falling in the storm.

A blink of an eye, and all things pass.

TO THAT ROOM

And I return to that town,
to that house,
to that room,
the bones of the dead beneath me;
they know me
though I do not know them.

I'm surrounded by the books and papers
of other dead;
I know them
though they do not know me.

This earth: the remains of strangers
naturalized by death.

I return
because one must return,
because the dead must rise again.

HOME

Nothing but the nightmare bus
passes by our home.
And nothing but the whistle of a single train
sounds in our memory—
sometimes it takes our children,
sometimes it brings us colonizers.
Its whistle is the silence of victims,
its smoke is their history.
And in our sea, nothing
but a single ship casts anchor—
it brings colonizers
and escapes with victims.

What we feared came to pass.
What we hoped for never came.

DISSATISFIED

> *Nor do I claim that my own self is innocent, for the self commands man to do evil, unless my Lord bestows His grace, my most merciful and forgiving Lord.*
> —The Glorious Quran (12:53)

Dissatisfied with the walls filled with darkness,
with the tiny cracks
through which the light leaks out
in a memory that's shattered every time . . .

Who am I in all of this?
I lack the strength to ask.
I'm the prisoner of my self, it commands me
to do what my body cannot bear.

THE LAST DAY

The last day of an age,
the last page in a notebook,
the last lip,
the last finger,
the last thread of light,
the last bit of darkness.

IN DESPAIR

You recorded these words in the street,
between sleep and waking,
while crossing the valley of the shadow of death,
while telling yourself,
Don't be afraid.
You recorded them
between one glance and another,
in the cracking of breath,
in the ease and bluster
of an extravagance that tells time,
"I *am* time."
You recorded them in despair as well,
in boredom's embrace,
while disappointment
was raised in the glasses.
You recorded them
in the swarms of pretenders,
at the banquet of disgrace,
and in the overflowing of the void.

You recorded these words
to no avail.

A DISTANT COUNTRY

How many bedrooms do I need
to get a bit of sleep?
How many chairs
to sit myself down?
How many roads
to walk back to you,
my distant country?
This time I've gone
and I'm not coming back.
Your job, now, is to slip out,
lovesick and afraid,
and come in search of me.

WE NEVER STOP

I have no country to return to,
no country to be banished from,
a tree whose roots
are a running river:
It dies if it stops,
it dies if it doesn't.

On the cheeks and arms of death
I spent the best of my days,
and the land I lost each day
I gained each day anew.
The people had a single country,
but mine multiplied in loss,
renewed itself in absence.
Its roots, like mine, are water:
If it stops it withers,
if it stops it dies.
Both of us are running
with a river of sunbeams,
a river of gold dust
that rises from ancient wounds,
and we never stop.
We keep on,
never thinking to pause
so our two paths can meet.

I have no country to be banished from,
no country to return to:
I'll die if I stop,
I'll die if I keep going.

From *Discourses*

He said to me:[12]
It's true that my heart, on the day
of the Battle of Badr,
was with the Messenger and the believers,
yet I couldn't keep it from being moved
by the singing of the songstresses
and the chanting of the Quraysh
and the way Abu Jahl was dancing
with the sword—
his seventy years couldn't keep him
from leaping, with his song, into battle,
though he didn't know that the thirsty dunes
would be watered with his blood
before the noontime arch was broken.
My son, the believers moved me with their faith,
and the infidels moved me
with their pride and refusal,
and I was with the one side
and the other,
and this was one
of the many tragedies
we never speak of
to anyone.

My son, the *Glory of Islam,* as all of you call it,
is a collection of so many wounds
and only pulses thanks to those wounds,
and I'm not one to cover them with heartfelt fervor
or empty rhetoric.
Go find someone else
to deny the state of things—
that our guidance and misguidance,
our good deeds and transgressions,
have blended in our hearts,
like clusters of grapes pressed out
into the earthen jugs.

He said to me:
Death pummels us,
shakes the foundations of our home,
strikes its cornerstones,
snuffs out the tiny lamps I light.

Death reminds us
we have a home.

He said to me:
I started in a city
and ended in a city
but never made it to Paradise.
He said to me: Look into my eyes
before you say you've arrived
in Paradise.
Paradise was brought into being
only to fall out of it.
This city
is Paradise enough for me.

He said to me:
I taught poetry for three years at a university,
and in all that time
I didn't write a single poem
that was pleasing to poetry's goddess,
and neither did my students.
Poetry's like nature—
knowledge is powerless before her,
and the teachers offer her their sacrifices
to no avail.

He said to me:
Sometimes I catch myself red-handed,
happy
in a new city,
surprising myself
in the company of friends,
or with a drink,
or even
with a bowl of lentil soup
in a simple cafeteria,
as if I hadn't woken in Carmel's Paradise
on the day God created
the heavens and the earth,
as if I hadn't spent
the past five and a half centuries
suffering the loss of Granada.

He said to me:
I cleaved my life in two
and further cleaved the halves,
to say nothing of the cleavings wrought
by invaders and tyrants,
by despair, and hope, and urban devastation.
I've only ever seen my life in tatters,
fractured like clouds,
though from time to time it pulls itself together
to rain down—
that's why, no matter where I'm exiled,
there will be flowers
and verdant fields.

He said to me:
We were scattered
like strange birds in a strange forest,
and from our wanderings came poets and singers
who wrote and composed us as flocks
and formed a nation out of us.
But here we are now,
lost once again.

He said to me:
"Every soul shall have a taste of death."[13]

Not mine.
It keeps tossing back its drink
and will not die.

He said to me:
I don't want to die in an occupied country,
or have my name appear
in occupied newspapers,
or have the bell of an occupied church
ring for me,
or have mourners pray over me
in an occupied mosque—
if I'm lucky, that is, and the occupiers
do not steal my body.

From *You Are Not a Poet in Granada*

RISE, GRANADA

I

Rise, Granada,
over the pages of the downcast country
and the somber inkwell,
over this eternity filled with sorrow.
Rise, Granada,
for the words of the hour have no sun,
rise, lost one,
over those who believe they are not lost,
and rise on those who *were* lost
though none of them were put
on the lists of the missing.
Rise over a man within the colony
in whose heart the blood has dried,
over a bus of horror that never stops,
rise over it
as it stops, suddenly, at the door of our home.
Should I be the first passenger?
Or should I,
with a cry,

rip up
all of this?

Am I so lost
to think of the sun as the name of some lost city
and to make everything I do well a stopping point
for those who lost it
and those who brought it back,
while eternity
and endlessness
move pawns on the chessboard?

Am I so lost
to neither see nor hear,
to bequeath all that I do well
to your loss?

Rise, Granada,
over this eternity filled with sorrow
and this endless tragedy,
and everything between them.

II

Rise, Granada, over the downcast body,
and pour down
as love pours from the sky
without the earth knowing,
as the sky descends to earth
without either of them knowing.
And so it is they meet
as if for the very first time.

Rise, Granada,
for our meeting now is a miracle,
and it's as if I've traveled to you
on the back of a Buraq,
and it's as if we were walking now, together,
on the surface of the water.

III

Rise, Granada,
over the ailing river, and lean over its grasses,
for the river, as you know, is a body made
of water and mud,
and it's run by dreams, just like us,
and just like us, delusions push it
past its limits.

IV

Rise, Granada,
over the body hanging at the mouth of time.
Time never kissed it,
and it never flowed with time.
Rise in the distance,
for the distant one alone
can rise.

V

Rise, Granada,
over despair and hope, two children
playing in the courtyard of my home.

I married life
but I don't know who murdered her.
She left me my two children,
and I want them to grow up
so despair can gather strength
and the wind can brush the hair of hope.

Rise, Granada,
for these two children need your sun
more than they need a crippled father.

VI

Rise, Granada,
over this body that's cracked
like your great tower
(it forgot to factor in
the weight of time).
Here I am, just like it, sealing my archways with stones
and bidding farewell to this play of light and shadow.

YOU ARE NOT A POET IN GRANADA

When I found myself forgotten on your streets
I knew I had also found my city.
I told myself: a man
is not a prophet in his city,
and you
are not a poet in Granada.
Like a boy who struggles for twenty years
alone in his room
to gain a foothold at the lowest rungs of verse,
I must struggle in your rooms
without your knowing me.
You're like my country—seldom has it seen me,
yet it acquainted me with oblivion
and rocked my bed with it
until oblivion became my home.

My joy, today, is to be forgotten
as the wind forgets a pomegranate tree
in one of your gardens.

I WRITE THE LAND

I want to write the land,
I want the words
to be the land itself.
But I'm just a statue the Romans carved
and the Arabs forgot.
Colonizers stole my severed hand
and stuck it in a museum.
No matter. I still want to write it—
the land.
My silence is my story,
and my words are everywhere.

A NEW NOTEBOOK

All this dread
of a new notebook?
All this fear
of your own handwriting?
Here you are now
breaking fear with words
with lines devoid of dots and commas
You break it
when you yourself are broken

YOU SAY THAT

You say that dawn is refreshing and bountiful:
Like you, it rises
from time immemorial
anew,
as if it were the first dawn,
as if it were the last.

I HUNT THE BREEZE

I hunt the breeze in Granada's virgin summer
(it's the middle of May),
I hunt it, but the breeze knows
that my nets are all in tatters
(they're the unkempt hair of the days)
and that the air passes through my words
without seeing them.

Perhaps only we can see it—the language
of the people of Paradise?
Perhaps we've passed out of existence
without knowing it?
Perhaps the breeze itself
is a child in Paradise?

AS A VAGABOND

"Beauty lived as a vagabond"[14]
and still does.
Yesterday beauty told me
it was still looking
for a room or a fragment of a dream,
for a forgotten brother and a lost friend
and a family that changed their names and fled,
it told me it had been cured by oblivion
but has not forgotten—
it has no choice but to bear
the boulder of remembrance
from one place to the next.

"Beauty lived as a vagabond,"
and it's still sleeping
on the sidewalks,
and under bridges,
and in public parks.
And no one knows it. No one
knows that it's beauty.

READING *UYOUN AL-AKHBAR* IN THE LANGUAGE ACADEMY'S LIBRARY [15]

"He's more sinful than time—
caravans of errancy come to him,
and even the Recorder of Days
can't count all his sins."

How you would like to be him—
that libertine
whose life Ibn Qutaybah narrated.

IN THE CAFÉ

The buck gazes at the doe,
the doe glances at the buck.
He sings a flamenco for her,
she dances a bolero for him.
This play starts over
every day
with a new name,
with a name that repeats itself.
"Instinct," the schoolbooks say,
"emotions," and the poems bat their eyes.
But this won't change a thing.
The fact is
that the buck is courting the doe now,
and the doe is thinking
of binding him by the horns
with a chain of roses.

IN THE LIE

I

Age was a pair of doves,
and we let it fly.

II

I'll keep after summer
until I've forestalled his pretexts and lies,
I'll keep after him
and he'll keep after me—
summer and a man
telling each other lies.

THE WATER DOESN'T REMEMBER

Take refuge in language:
It's the only solid ground
for ships pitched by waves of misfortune.
Take refuge in language:
It often took refuge in you
to vent all its passions,
a snake seeking shelter from the flames
within the flames,
a man running from one lion
into the jaws of another.
Take refuge in the words of the forefathers,
for the words of your contemporaries
cannot comfort a wound
or prevent a suicide
or stop these poison gases
that drive you from your home
and ruin your place of exile.
From city to city you lost your life,
and you remain
with a wealth of losses.
I saw you lose,
I heard you lose,
I touched, tasted, smelled your losses, as I had never
touched, smelled, or tasted before—
as if the senses were made for this.
The sun of loss rises over your life
and calls itself an Andalus,
and your days flow in the Darro river:
The water doesn't remember
a family, doesn't hear

the voice of a friend,
and has no sense for justice.
Your memory flows through the water
but you don't follow it
to the river's mouth;
it doesn't even know
that it's your memory.

The sun of loss rises
while your days roar in silence.

I KNOW THIS SEA

I know this Mediterranean,
I know all the lies of its waves.
I know how it led migrants and refugees astray
and named them the drowned,
I know how it made us as heartless
as the sea itself.

I want to fall upon it with the full force
of my cry—
I want it to know
that *I* know.

LIGHTNING WRITES POETRY

Lightning never sits down at a table
to write poetry,
yet it is poetry's only embodiment.
It lights up the whole universe
then disappears.
What poet hasn't dreamed
of becoming lightning?

IN RABAT'S NIGHT

Two Gnawa musicians passed by,
one was plucking the *guembri,*
the other was playing the *krakeb*
while his smile did the singing.

An African smile
singing
in Rabat's night.

Black caravans light up the night with their soft singing
between Ghana and Timbuktu.

A singing that fades
while history turns in its sleep.
Were we dreaming?
Or were we simply caught
in Rabat's night?

I WON'T GO BACK

I feel a yearning to abandon this home,
to abandon this love,
to leave my memory as a boy leaves his parents' home,
proclaiming, "I won't go back, not even
if I have to sleep on the streets while the whole world
    is burning—
I won't go back."

I forestall the home's yearning
to abandon me,
the city's yearning to evict me.
I have no home, no city.
But the vastness of exile—that, at least, is mine.

AN AFTERNOON IN ALBAICÍN

News of your death reached me
one sweltering afternoon
as I sat with friends on a peak of Albaicín.
They said, "your death."
I said, "your life."

A hand of snow emerges from the void
and lands a punch, every time.

We were passing the time talking
about East and West
when death came to a peak of Albaicín.
So death reached Granada too
with a message on the phone.
Death rode in on its black horse
and took a friend
while the hooves wounded the sunset
over the "summer palace" of Alhambra.
I didn't try to stop it—
we Arabs don't stop death,
we just want it to know the value
of the hand that slackens the reins.

We refrained from the golden sunset's bullion,
from the pearls of the wounds,
and the emerald of the virgin gaze,
while seeking solace
on a sweltering afternoon in Albaicín.

AN ALGERIAN *NUBA*[16]

And he poured me the second cup,
Leave me, friend, leave me.
And he poured me the tenth cup,
Leave me, friend, leave me.
I lost my share of grace,
while my share of hell lies before me,
Leave me, friend, leave me.
I lost the way to my country,
though the only thing I know
is the way to my country,
Leave me, friend, leave me.
Your cup contains oblivion,
so leave me,
and if love asks after us, say,
Leave me, leave me.
The waves of the sea
have neither eyes nor ears,
and the boats took your family and mine,
Leave me, friend, leave me.
And pour me the second cup,
and pour me the tenth,
and leave me, friend,
leave me.

FROM ONE COUNTRY TO ANOTHER

You lose your pens from one country to another,
your ink as well,
and you too are lost as you wait for an olive branch
in the flood of words.

You're lost, and no one's there
to save you.
The crow, the dove—
they've gone now
and taken the olive branch with them.

EARLY RISER[17]

"Rise early for delights, ride out to them,
early to play and early to joy,
before the forenoon's sun has sipped the morning rain
from the mouths of the chrysanthemums."

As for me, I always rose early
for my own death.

A MORNING NOTE FOR
THE PARADISE OF CARMEL

I

What are you?
The ghost of a dead lover?
A garden that abandonment bought
before locking its door?
It would be foolish to call you my place of exile
after so much intimacy.

II

But I've settled within you
and become an exile
at the same time.
I'm no different from *any* prisoner,
except that I hide my prison as best I can
and do not have the luxury
of waiting for freedom.

III

My freedom lies
in *all* people
finding their freedom.

I HEARD HIM SING

This poem was written for a man
whose country was destroyed
and who gave me
the little that was left in his hands.
"Possess nothing, and nothing possesses you,"
as the proverb goes.
From the depths of destruction, I heard him sing:
"You, passing by the mills when the water's been cut off."[18]

Water, electricity, hope—
they were all cut off.

IN THE COLONY

How do we spend our lives in the colony?
Cement blocks and thirsty crows
are the only things I see.

Freedom's a statue made of clay
cracking beneath the coastal sun
and the songs do not know it.
It's best not to tell
the woman waiting in the corridor
that her child has passed away in the ICU.

What should we do in this country of ours
which has become a colony?

I DON'T CLAIM

I

I don't claim to have any enemies
other than myself,
my demanding
melancholic
self
that sleeps on its bed of misery,
always ready to spill its blood
over the smallest of trifles—
leaving nothing
for my enemies to do.

I don't claim to have any enemies
other than myself.

II

I don't claim to have any friends
other than myself,
and I'm not denying anything
since the ones I'm offering my spot to
are also myself,
which I'm splitting into many selves
and losing one by one,
just as man loses himself—
I don't claim
to have any friends at all.

III

I don't claim to have a companion
other than this wandering shadow:
When it walks on the land, you call it a dream,
and when it walks on its head, you call it delusion.
I don't claim to have any companions
but it—my dream, my delusion,
my sweet death every night.

IV

I don't claim to have a family
beyond the ones I lost in wars,
the ones I lost to exile
in the paradise of contentment,
and in hell.

I don't claim to have any family
but the ones with mislaid graves
and well-known places of exile,
the ones murdered on the coasts
and waiting at the borders.

I don't claim to have any family
but my own.

V

I don't claim to have a country.
My country is an Andalus of poems and water,
I lost it,
I'm *still* losing it—
in loss
it becomes my country.

I don't claim to have any country
other than loss.

THE COUNTRY CONTRABASS

My grandmother was a great musician,
no one played the country contrabass like her.
In spite of death
and the leveling of hills
I can still see her standing there
plucking, with impossible tenderness
her massive contrabass.

(Her music, now,
has become a piece of time.)

All I can do is stand here and play,
because she too is still playing.

A BRIEF COMMENTARY ON
"LITERARY SUCCESS"

Here in my prison cell, which I chose
of my own free will,
here between the mountain and the sea,
this is where the news reaches me,
the news of my poetry spreading like fire.
And there are some who congratulate me
that the flames have reached
the ends of the earth.

These ashes that were once my body,
that were once my country—
are they supposed to find joy
in all of this?

THE INTERROGATION

You have nothing to say
in the morning interrogation,
but Creation's enforcer insists on some words
that he can take from you,
and you tell him:
"Write whatever you want on my page—
here's my signature
on a blank piece of paper."

I BEAR ONLY SMOKE

Adonis "bears the harvest of the East to the West."
As for me,
I bear nothing but bad news,
which should have reached you
four centuries ago.

Fire has spread through the harvest,
and I, like the wind, bear nothing but smoke.

Smoke, and bad news—
your harvest from the East.

I REMEMBER UMAR[19]

In these days when we have nothing left
I remember Umar.
Back then the people of Jerusalem didn't know
who was the Caliph and who the servant,
since the two took turns
riding a single camel.
And it delights me to see his young helper
turning toward the city walls,
while the Caliph leads his camel on, loosening the reins
and praising God's greatness.
What joy the young helper must have felt
while the Caliph was serving him . . .

In Granada I found myself standing in the slaughter.
The Alhambra saying one thing, the displaced
were saying another.
Who uproots the people?
Who drives them, under pain of death,
to the "land of the enemy"?
I remembered Umar,
the Arab who led the stars with the reins of his camel,
and I breathed in all the aromas
of the perfumers' souq,
like people multiplying,
changing,
becoming neighbors.
Without them, walking through the souq
would be no prayer.

I said to myself: Thank Umar,
for without him, you wouldn't be standing here now,
and Jerusalem wouldn't have gathered its people
to blossom in its shade.
Thank the bedouin who led civilization with the reins of
  his camel,
thank the bedouin who forged civilization with words
  of conscience,
thank the man who opened the city and never closed it,
thank the man who never displaced or uprooted anyone,
thank Umar, who, fourteen centuries after his death,
is still granting safety to the people of Aelia
and still granting *you* safety as well,
thank him for the proximity of Isabella's slaughters
and the great flame of the Andalusians,
thank him with a stolen heart and tearful eyes,
and try, just try
to stop him
as he leads the stars with the reins of his camel.

AS IF TALKING TO MYSELF

A dead poet sat down beside me
and talked to me as if he were talking to himself:
"You can only conceive of heaven
when you are in hell."

So let my country be hell's heaven,
and let hell's heaven be my country.
I too am a dead poet
talking to you
as if talking to myself.

CITIZENS OF THE *TRISTES TROPIQUES*

I've always been moved
by Levi-Strauss's title.
Is it because I've imagined the Tropics
of Capricorn and Cancer
passing by, hunched over with grief?
Or because grief touches
the recurring fates of poets
without a second thought?
What sad fate do you bring back, poet?
What fate are you repeating?
Who are we waiting for
to grant us salvation?
Hasn't the time come for a collective scream,
each from their own place of exile:
Revoke our citizenship
in the *Tristes Tropiques.*

OUT OF THE DEPTHS

Out of the depths I cry to you, O Lord.[20]

As for me, I've got no depths left
from which to cry.
Lord, give me back my cry.
It was never mine,
it belongs to others,
and they will be asking for it.
I've got no depths left
from which to call to you.
Walls beyond walls,
while reunion waves
the cloth of separation.
A face is racked with darkness,
and your wrongs are great, O depths.
Walls beyond walls,
while separation waves
the cloth of reunion.

Faces, walls—
the cry does not descend to them,
and the depths fail
to rise to meet them.

FOREVER ROAMING

I was leading my own funeral,
roaming the borders of this land,
the sacred, the profane,
the ones floating on its wound.
I spent hours, maybe years, roaming.
I reached Jerusalem shortly before sunset
and climbed the hill.
The mourners didn't notice me,
I watched while the diggers
lowered the coffin,
and as they headed back
I slipped a few bills into one of their hands.

What once was tragic
now seemed insignificant.
What once was unimportant
now rent the heart with a jagged knife.

I asked the Lord my God,
"Is it all over . . . ?"
And He replied, "No.
You will roam and roam
before you rest."

A CONVERSATION WITH FARIS BAROUD'S MOTHER IN THE AL-SHATI CAMP[21]

She said to me: "My boy, Lord knows I don't like lying,
but sometimes I *do* lie,
may God forgive me.
When I visited Faris the last time, I pretended I could see—
I didn't want to upset him.
On that day I climbed almost fifty stairs.

"After that visit . . . I went to see him again,
but they turned me away.
'No more visits,' they said,
and now fifteen years have passed.
I want to see him and hug him
before I die.
It's true my eyes have lost their sight,
but my heart
has a sight all its own . . . "

Then she sang:
Curse the door of the prison
and the door's maker.
My boy, my boy—
cut off from the fresh air,
cut off from his beloveds.

In my prison, now—my vast one,
which is not so different from yours—
all I can hear
is the sound of her singing.

TAKE ME, DRAG ME AWAY

And a strong white horse drags his reins
to the water, for death has taken
the one who used to give him water.
—From the self-elegy of Malik Ibn al-
Rayb al-Tamimi (circa 638–677 CE)[22]

Take me, drag me away,
far from both of you.

Is this the "Jerusalem"
who caused me so much misery?

Take me, drag me away,
far away from her.

As for the strong white horse that drags his reins,
the settlers left no one to give him water.

Take me, drag me away,
far from my memory.

LAND

Land, how much misery
you've brought to your people.
They're wretched when they have you,
wretched when they lose you.

Land, if only
we could inhabit the clouds.

THE SHELLING ENDED

No one will know you tomorrow.
The shelling ended
only to start again within you.
The buildings fell, the horizon burned,
only for flames to rage inside you,
flames that devour even stone.

The murdered are sunk in sleep,
but sleep will never find you—
awake forever,
awake until they crumble, these massive rocks
said to be the tears of retired gods.

Forgiveness has ended,
and mercy is bleeding outside of time.
No one knows you now,
and no one will know you tomorrow.
You, like the trees,
are planted in your place
while the shells are falling.

From *Exhausted
on the Cross*

MOUNT CARMEL [23]

Though you're right beside it
you can't call out to the sea:
Neighbor, come join me for a coffee.
Instead, and without my permission,
my other neighbor, Carmel,
visits me through the window,
never trying to enter by the door.
(It owns the place, at any rate.)

Sometimes the church bells reach me
from the depths of Wadi Nisnas;
and some mornings the call to prayer
comes in quietly from the Istiqlal Mosque (borne
on an ancient breeze from Wadi Salib);
and the Baha'is keep giving alms
and filling the city with Persian gardens
that escaped from Shiraz;
and in Kababir
the followers of Mirza Ghulam Ahmad
maintain their naps of devotion
and hunt for Truth in the Prophet's words;

as for the holy men among the Druze,
their poems reach me from the temple
at the foot of Mount Hermon
like the white headscarves of their women
(the ones that hide a thousand years of darkness).

And I, aimless
between the mountain and the sea,
I who follow no one but myself—
what am I doing among all these devotees
here
where time has found its end?

IN SHATILA

"There's no dignity here,"
the old woman tells you,
the one who left Haifa when she was nine months old.
She's sixty-five now
and standing in the swelter
outside her "house" in the camp.
She says it all
in just a couple of seconds.
She says it all
in just four words.

Rivers of regret,
years of agony that drown
in just four words.

You look at her bent back and think of the pines on
   Mount Carmel.
You look into her eyes and remember the kindness of
   the coast
while she complains to you about the faucets
and the brackish water that comes out of them.
And all you can do is smile as you open your heart
to this lovesick child.
You know you won't see her again:
She won't be there
when you head back to Haifa.

What did she tell you as she said her goodbyes?
What did you promise her as you said yours?

How could you smile, indifferent
to the brackish water of the sea
while the barbed wire wrapped around your heart?

How could you,
you son of a bitch?

ELEGY FOR A SLEEPING CHILD

I.

Son, I come from the memory
of the ones who've been killed—
it can't tell the difference
between a sleeping child
and a murdered child.
But you're still asleep, my son,
though the field's awake all around you in the painting.
And I'm still up, past midnight,
feeling sick in this cold northern land
and listening to the dark rain beating.
You're still asleep, and you can't hear the rain
or my misgivings.
Where can I find
such contented sleep?
The field's awake around you.
Like me, it's thinking
of your long sleep in the colors of the artist,
who covers you now
with a layer of dark air.

You're sleeping now
like a murdered child.

II.

The air's heavy in the painting,
and my eyes do not help me:

I don't have
the strength to see you.

Failing,
I surrender to the darkness.

BECAUSE OF A WOMAN

I came to this city
because of a casual date with a woman,
and now seven years have gone by.
And I crossed the bridge to that other city
because of a date with a woman (it, too, was casual).
Everywhere I've gone
was because of a woman.
And despite all my hollow claims that women are disloyal,
my guide was always a woman.
A woman gave birth to me,
and a woman grabbed my fingers and started writing
(and she's still writing, even after her death).
Every house I've ever lived in
was built by a woman
or owned by a woman
or lost by a woman.
My country's a woman,
and this mother goddess
whose streets I drag a cross through
is also a woman.
And in a past life, when my corpse lay out in the open
and they forbade them to bury me,
it was a woman who emerged from the shadows
to lay me in the earth.
When no one believed me,
a woman believed me,
and because of a woman
I lived life to the fullest.
It's regrettable that only men
will carry my coffin
this time around.

A SHORT STORY ABOUT
THE CLOSING OF THE SEA

When you turn down that street at the city's edge,
the one that leads to the camp,
if you see children leaving that school that resembles
    a prison,
if you see seven of them standing there, on the threshold of
    silence, watching,
if you see a slender child whose eyes are gleaming with all
    the world's promises,
you'll have found my friend Tayseer.
His family has a country that was stolen in broad daylight,
and you can see the vigilance of its birds in his
    anxious eyes.
The cement houses,
the memories of tin sheets,
the voices that were fearful
of the occupying army's transceivers
through the long weeks of curfew—
none of this has taken the slightest spark from his eyes.
He saw the sea once, and nothing can convince him
he won't see it again.
"When the curfew's lifted, we'll take you to the sea"—
that's how they used to comfort him.
And when the curfew finally *was* lifted one evening,
    they said,
"The sea's closed now, go to sleep."
He didn't sleep that night. He imagined an old man
who closed the sea by lowering a massive tin sheet that
    stretched from the star on the horizon to the sand on
    the shore:

The man secured it with a huge padlock,
then went back to his home (the padlock was larger
than the one on Tayseer's father's shop on Omar
   Mukhtar street).

When you walk down that street at the city's edge
(the one that leads to the camp),
if you see two eyes gleaming with all the world's promises,
ask them, I beg you, if the Gaza Sea has "opened" yet,
or if it's still closed.

EXHAUSTED ON THE CROSS

The ones hanging
are tired,
so bring us down
and give us some rest.

We drag histories behind us
here
where there's neither land
nor sky.

Lord,
sharpen your knife
and give your sacrifice its rest.

* * *

You had no mother or father
and you never saw your brothers
hanging
from the cold talons of dawn.
You loved no one,
and no one ever abandoned you,
and death never ate from your hands.
You cannot know our pain.

* * *

I'm not King David—
I won't sit at the gate of regret
and sing you psalms of lamentation
after the sins.

* * *

Bring me down,
let me have my rest.

ENOUGH

For Y. H.[24]

I have so many friends
sleeping in tombs from different ages—
at night I tell them stories,
more often than I should.

It's for this reason—you who, repulsed by life,
are speeding to your death—
that I want you alive,
that I want to be the one who leaves
this time around.
Come tell me stories and stay
above the ground. I've company enough already
beneath it.

Pull back, now, from this path of carnage—
enough is enough.

ALL OF IT

Carriages drawn by cheerful horses
and the tunes of accordions,
or sullen buses
and relatives weeping at their doors—
it's all a journey, dear,
and here we are now, back from it.

I name it earth, and am not ashamed.
It's all earth.
It's all death.
All of it.

MY DEFEATED BANNER

If I could come back,
I wouldn't come under any other banner.
I'd still embrace you
with two severed hands.
I don't want wings in paradise,
I just want your graves by the river.
I want eternity at the breakfast table
with the bread and oil.
I want *you*—
earth,
my defeated banner.

"A Breeze from Üsküdar" and Other Poems

BOY

Boy,[25]
walk on the days' brow.
Their brow is broad—the people call it life.
Walk there and leave your troubles behind.
It's better to go barefoot,
since most people (as you know) are prisoners of
   their shoes,
and you don't want to be imprisoned by anything.
Walk gently,
for the days are the brow of a sleeping creature,
and, despite the rumors of their cruelty—
they always appreciate some kindness.
Don't cross life, and never tread on the days' brow
except with two bare feet.

Boy,
sing your song in the voice of your choosing,
spread it upon the earth, present it to the people—
your song only becomes your own
when it leaves you.

Boy,
do you recall when we entered love's gambling den
one dawn without our parents knowing?
It was the first of many losses.
There was nothing we didn't gamble,
nothing we didn't lose.
We pitied the winners:
they left burdened with their cowardice,
while we left crowned in laurel.
You were so skilled at twisting
Al-Niffari's *Station of the Sea:*
"gambling holds all salvation,"
"the one who sets sail without wagering everything . . .
    perishes,"
"the one who is saved . . . perishes,"
"the one who *thinks* he has been saved . . . perishes,"
and "the one who thinks he's *najwan*—a survivor—
    also perishes."

Boy,
your notebook's out of pages,
and life's nothing but a notebook,
so replace your notebook with another,
your life with another,
since lives—like meanings—are strewn along the road.

Boy,
you lived and died,
and the days were a broad brow you stitched with two
    bare feet
and two bare hands,
and words were your only offering

to gods who fled from their temples
in horror of the One God,
just as words were your only offering
to the lonely peoples
who also fled in horror—
but for some reason you cannot fathom
the One God did not save them.

WITNESSING ABANDONMENT

The cruelty of witnessing abandonment
as it eats from your shoulder
while you stand there like a statue
from some bygone civilization—
unable to speak a single word
against abandonment.

WHILE SPEAKING ABOUT
AN EARTHQUAKE IN ISTANBUL

Even if the earthquake comes while I'm here
and I survive,
as I always survive,
I'll still clean up the rubble with the people
and build the new homes alongside them,
I'll be a little less angry—
at least *that* destruction will be
from our Mother Earth,
and not from colonial planes
piloted by bastards.

ABANDONMENT AND A HOME

You did to me what abandonment does to a home,
what a home does to abandonment,
and I had done all this
to myself before—
most likely, I am both
abandonment
and a home.

You did to me what the flowers do to spring,
and I did to you what the spring does to flowers.

So let each of us judge our actions
according to their conscience.

NURTURED BY THE HAND OF GOD

He told me: Love is no less dangerous than hate.
Just ask me, I who am destroyed
by my love each day,
and within each gesture and feeling.

Hate's destruction
falls on its owner like a ruined wall
and kills or disfigures him.
As for love's destruction, it, like nature,
is nurtured by the hand of God.

LATE

I'll be late to Hell.
I know Charon will ask for a permit
to board his boat.
Even there
I'll need a Schengen visa.

LIKE EVERYONE ELSE

Time lays waste to you
in the long rut of days.
This is the truth you're running from,
like everyone else.
In the rut of time the days lay waste to you,
though you imagine it's *you* laying waste to *them,*
in the rut of this short life in which you're garrisoned—
a soldier who lost his war with time
and who's finding it hard
to raise a white flag.

THE DAY LEAVES YOU

The day leaves you in the carriages of the sun,
which is setting somewhere,
you've become so used to this
that it no longer hurts.

Night passes near you like some deaf beast
(it has nothing to do
with the night the singers praise).
It passes near
but does not see you.

IN RESPONSE TO A POET
WHO DREAMS OF GLORY

And do not think that glory lies in rising early.
Glory lies in sleeping and dreaming,
it's also glorious to pass away
and graciously leave
your demise behind.
All glory lies in this: to die
as a human being.

A BREEZE FROM ÜSKÜDAR

Treetops are swaying among the tiled roofs,
and your writing chair made of reed,
it too was once branches
swaying in the wind,
and here you are looking at them,
surrendering yourself completely
to what the breeze from Üsküdar wants
as it blows in, preceding
the muezzin's inflections and chanting.
And you think that you are happy here,
delighted to be waking up
on this exquisite afternoon,
surrendered completely
to a breeze from Üsküdar.

SOUSAN'S MIRROR

In your mirror, Sousan,
I saw my face this morning
with Carmel's pines and a blue patch of sky
behind it.
The past and the future were running together
like a boy and a girl,
and I saw you,
and I saw myself—
we too were running
and no one could catch us.

Lost, the poet on his way to wild roses,
lost on the way to the laurel,
lost in the henna blossom,
lost in the *muwashah,* and lost in the *tarjī'-band,*
lost in wafting and reverberation
and in the quivering of a candle above a river,
lost in the nape of a gazelle,
and in a necklace, and in an earring's shadow,
lost on the way to death,
lost in ambergris and agarwood and musk,
lost in the suns of pomegranate blossoms
and in the unrest of the bitter orange,
lost, the poet, in the carnelian,
in the voice of the reader of *maqāms,*
lost in Nishapur, lost in Samarkand,
and like him, I, too, have lost the way.

SLEEP

Sleep,
for the tablet of fate will soon be broken
and the angels will fall like snow
from this sullen sky, and your smile will embrace all
   of existence,
while you think back on a few thousand years
and forgive them.

From *Weary of Walking in the Barzakh*

I OFTEN DREAM

I often dream that the waves of Haifa's sea
are dunes of blue
and that an ageless camel driver
is emerging from them,
dragging the days behind him.
He stops, for a little while, beneath my window
so I can give him everything
the Arabs have laid away with me:
the openings of unrecited poems
and wars that never ended.
I give him all of it,
all their desperate love.

And as he's loading these troves onto his steed
I convince him to take my life as well,
for which I've found no city,
and my city,
for which I've found no life.
And I wave to him as he cuts across the dunes of blue,
returning with his haul.

My joy is indescribable:
The Mediterranean
has become a sea of dunes.

AT A POETRY FESTIVAL

In front of each poet was the name of their country,
but in front of me
there was only "Jerusalem."

How ghastly your name is, my little country,
your name is all I have left,
I sleep in it
and wake with it.
Your name's like a ship with no hope of arriving,
no hope of returning. . . .

It never arrives, and it never returns.
It never arrives, and it never goes under.

BUILDINGS

I often laughed at myself
since I was only ever in buildings
that were half-inhabited,
half-deserted,
the moment the shelling came.

And, as if this weren't enough, I found myself
with someone else's bags
and someone else's life,
taking a shower on a bus
that was now in a different country.
Was I a dead man
to look for my bags with such desperation?

We will not end,
not even when the planes finish
razing the buildings to the ground.

I SAW TREES

I saw trees walking with me at dawn
to the gates of the consulates,
their hands full of immigration forms.
I pretended not to see them,
they pretended not to see me.

I saw trees
gathering their roots in baskets
and sitting, haphazardly, in boats,
at the mercy of the waves,
at the mercy of the smugglers.

I saw trees moving toward me
and I was there,
deliriously pointing at their dead branches.

I saw all this,
but no one believed me.

A VISITOR FROM HELL

A resident of Hell, I've been sitting here,
Lord,
for years.
Do I not deserve
to be a citizen?
How is it that even in Hell
the homes have owners collecting rent
and tenants being evicted?
We used to think that Hell
meant being stable, the end of displacement.
(In truth, we imagined it as a prison
with no NGOs to decry the acts of torture,
where the angels were executioners
immune from all accountability.)
But here we are now, and there's none of that.
Who would believe that even in Hell
I'd be sitting here, my hand on my cheek,
waiting for salvation?

* * *

Heaven and Hell,
I lived them both so many times,
until Heaven was no longer Heaven,
Hell no longer Hell.
I grew weary of walking in the Barzakh,
yesterday I imagined it as a dark shore
while I plunged, barefoot,
into the hollowest of waves,
carrying sandals

for the days beyond the Barzakh.
The sea was a marvel of darkness,
and I was like a man facing his fate
with sandals in his hands.

* * *

Tonight I can't find the courage
to go down to the Barzakh.
Better to sleep, I told myself,
and visit my dead family—
they're the only ones now
who might open their doors
to a visitor from Hell.

A FLEETING SLAUGHTER

Eternity doesn't concern me in the slightest.
I wake to a fleeting slaughter
and emerge from a worn-out nightmare.
My only ties are with the land, with the transparency
of the evening above a stolen country.
I avoid looking at the sea,
just as the fox
avoids looking at its wounded leg.

THIS DARKNESS

A sentence about this darkness in which I lived
and from whose solid stones I built my days.
I kept on climbing
until I myself became the darkness.

THE NEW YEAR

In the New Year's fireworks and their sounds
I see Baghdad's sky lit up by shells
on the night of the invasion,
I see the way Gaza,
with its amputated limbs,
bears witness to a New Year
every afternoon,
I see Syrians running
with no sky above them
and no star to guide them.

A few minutes later, the fireworks fall silent.
The people have their New Year now.

As for our year—
the war's already consumed it.

IN CAPTIVITY

In the beginning a person's a prisoner of his body,
a prisoner of this vast dirt,
and every captivity after that is easy.

NO ONE

No one's said what I've said
and had the land let them go.

I'm trying, now, to go about my business,
but she keeps handing me
the rags of her dead father,
the picture of her lost son
and her kidnapped son
and the son who sold her.

Endless caravans of slaves,
endless stories of injustice—
she keeps placing them in front of me,
and I cannot get away.

The land
won't let me go.

THE THIEVES

The thieves were stealing sheep and gold,
and I heard of a man whose wife they stole,
of people whose wallets and cars were stolen.
But who believes me when I say that my country,
with its mountains and sea,
with its blue sky,
with its villages that God inhabited, one
after the other—
who believes me when I say
that it, too, was stolen?

TAKE THIS WALTZ

The waltz of my night moves
between the *muwashahāt* of Sabah Fakhri
and the rhythms of Abdel Wahab.[27]
There's someone shooting from the window
and someone wielding death by water
or death by fire.
Jerusalem itself collapses,
but the waltz doesn't stop,
not even when the burning pillars of history
crumble all around me,
not even when I see
little Zionists
playing thieves
pretending to be Zionists,
so small
they're almost invisible.

Take it,
take this waltz away from me.

HILLS OF THORNS

I hear those women lamenting within me:
"Oh, how long you've been walking
barefoot in the wilds."
Like them, I cross the land of nightmares without return,
wilds of thorns that have no end,
I cross them like a grouse,
without return,
without return.

Like them, I too
become a thorn
in these hills of thorns.

A CITY QUARTET

I

Doors and walls
and windows,
a human life:
a city.

II

He used to sleep like everyone else
but wake up differently.
He came and went
yet never left his place.

III

Where do they lead?
The gates?
The outlets?
The washrooms?
Where exactly do the latter lead?

IV

Doors that no one enters,
windows that no one looks through:

How have you become *my* doors
and *my* windows?
How has abandonment
become the keeper of orchards
I do not own?
And how has ruin preceded me
to a city I cannot find?

SOMEONE THERE

Books and dust, and chairs, and broken lamps,
cushions, desks, and endless sheets of paper,
old clothes, towels, sheets,
bags of all kinds and sizes,
a folded handmade rug,
a plundered carpet, and a borrowed one,
and the inlaid boxes of bridesmaids (filled
with unpaid bills instead of jewels):
twenty years of memories without much meaning,
twenty years of journeys, also
without much meaning.

Someone there
has wasted his life.

I'VE OFTEN TOLD YOU

I've often told you,
and while I was telling you, men were molding nations
   from their deaths,
and eternity was swaying
like a ship that's just discovered the sea.
I've often told you,
and while I was telling you, I was molding my death.
I've often told you, clay figure,
but when has the clay ever listened?
Who was the potter mocking
as he molded two large ears that could not hear?
Who was he mocking?
And why did he mold you a heart as well?
You flow out when you weep
till nothing's left of you but words.
I'm walking upon you now,
walking upon my death.
But would you believe that colonizers came from beyond
   the seas and stole you?
O clay, they took my death from me.

* * *

The forests are burning, the birds are leaving,
and our grandmothers, long gone, are turning over
in your embrace, O clay.
Who are you to bear all this?

* * *

Here you are, O clay,
sitting by Carmel's pines and sea
on a Thursday afternoon in the mountain's winter.
You've lived enough
to sit down now
and let yourself weep.

BREAKING DISHES

I return from that morgue
where suffering's embalmed
and feel nothing.
That's not my hand,
and that's someone else's heart.
But these eyes are mine,
and their agony knows no end.

A VARIATION ON A VERSE BY AL-MA'ARRI[28]

> *My body's a rag that will be woven*
> *into the mortal dirt.*
> *O Weaver of Worlds, weave me.*
> —Abu Al-'Ala Al-Ma'arri

My body's a blue the heavens forgot,
an orchard that fled from the spring.
O Weaver of Worlds,
what harm would be done
if you didn't weave me?

AFTER YOU'VE WORKED LIKE A SLAVE

After you've worked like a slave for sixteen long hours,
what poetry's left for you write?
Laid low on an awful bed
with an awful air conditioner above you
in this place that cannot even be
a place of exile—all this
for the sake of your venerable country.
Blessed are those whom no country makes wretched,
those who have never had a country cross their minds.
Blessed are the cows and the sheep
and all the earth's livestock.
And you tell me, O dutiful slave,
that you want to write poetry?

Write it, then. Write that now you're here
being flayed
in a different kind of slavery.

FROM THE VOID

This is speech
on the utmost, the ultimate,
and as you skid, terrified, through the twists and turns,
look for your face in an ancient room
and bring your journey back from the void.

SANĀSIL

I'm thinking now
of why the retaining walls between our gardens,
the ones we call *sanāsil,*
are collapsing
like tired men,
like women
who've had enough.

The walls are collapsing—if only
we could collapse like them.

THE RIVER

Weary, every day,
of never staying the same.

I SAID I'D RUN

I said I'd run to sleep,
I'd wake from the nightmare.
However long they search for me, they'll find nothing
but the story of a ghost that slipped like a thread from
   the story.

I'll run from all of this,
I'll wake up from it all.

THE LAST MASK

I haven't found it
yet:
the writing that liberates,
that I once grabbed hold of
while stumbling in those suburbs,
that resembles passion
and youth
and the delights of the flesh
in the way it surprises.

I haven't found it
and maybe I'll stop looking,
for I'm busy with trifles,
and my knife is dull, and I keep pretending
I have no time to sharpen it.
Time put on its masks
and called out
from behind the newborn's cradle,
the infant on all fours,
the child's first steps,
the stumbling adolescent,
the misgivings of the youth,
the grown man's despair.
Time called to me
from behind all the frail and aging promises
when it had no more masks to wear.

But now
I've got to crawl and walk and stumble

and chase down my misgivings
and lay myself in the coffin
in advance of all the promises.

The last mask is in my hands
and I will wear it now.

FOR THE SAKE OF SOME NEW TERROR

And since the time has come for the exiled to return
and for the one sleeping in the earth to rise,
isn't it also time, Lord, for all of this to end?
Lord, bring forth some new terror,
I'm weary of this nightmare
that's been on repeat
ever since You created me.
Start over, Lord,
and create me anew.

I'VE TRIED SO MANY TIMES

I've tried so many times to escape
but always you catch me off guard,
take me unawares,
as if I'd forgotten you a moment.

Whores from the Old Testament,
an orgy of woodwinds,
and the story repeats itself.

You take me unawares,
and there's no escaping your cross—
all I ever do is walk toward it.

PSALM

This is my body, breaking
for your sake,
so that the unforgivable
can be forgiven.
This is my body, breaking
in vain—
its only reward
is to be broken.

LITTLE MALTA[29]

The fog this morning is four thousand years old,
as is that woman passing beneath my window.

A little while ago
I stood in fog just like this
and saw a woman just like that
while my peers, laughing like real pirates,
hid plundered ships in our small bay,
for Haifa was coming to be called Little Malta.
You kind-hearted pirates whose greatest ambition is to
    please a woman,
whose greatest hope is a night when the lanterns are lit and
    the glasses are full,
you pirates for whom the sea is the lover of your mother,
    the land,
and life the wife of your father, death—
in a little while
empires will crash into each other like aging ships;
in a little while
invaders will land here, in tales of refugees;
in a little while
oblivion will descend like the fog at dawn
and swallow your voices and gestures and ropes;
in a little while
the pirates of cement mixers and atom bombs
will come ashore.

But I can pick out your laughter
from the depths of this oblivion,
while you return in plundered ships,

your greatest hope to please a woman. . . .
Which of you took my glass from the table?
Which of you drank it down?
And who is it
who's laughing now
as they whisper the words,
"To your health"?

A HAND ON A DESK

On a desk that was time
I placed my hand,
and it started writing of its own accord
(my hand occasionally left me
before returning wounded
and full of remorse).
Of its own accord it invents a story
and calls it mine:
Once upon a time there was a hand
on a desk writing its owner's story . . .
But after that, no one
heard anything about the hand, or its owner,
nor, of course, anything at all
about the writing desk.

TWO QUILLS

The quill of exhaustion
falls from on high
and cuts like a sword.
The quill of love
flies forever
in a discernible void.

A TRACE IN THE SAND

No one truly knows their footprints
before they've walked on the sand.

A man's startled that his steps leave traces
and delighted to leave behind
a trace the sands will soon erase.

A SONG FOR HELL

When I think of you, Hell,
I have to take a few steps back to my childhood,
stand in the yard and look at my family,
at wasted hills and a lost countryside,
and a fate abandoned to an evening of plunder and thieves.
And here you are, eating breakfast with us in our
   tiny kitchen.
You spent years with me
in schools that were worse than prisons.
Hell, you and water shaped existence itself.

And as I go searching for a country
the invaders stashed in their luggage
before they slipped away,
I find you there, on top of the bags,
but you don't extend your hand.
Hell,
my unruly child,
sit on your father's knees
and lay your head on this burning country—
your fate is like ours, abandoned
to an evening of plunder and thieves.

ROOMS

Horrible are your rooms, Lord,
horrible the houses raised by your servants,
horrible,
horrible,
and it's horrible that your rooms have become my life,
and this remorse, it too is horrible,
and this waking,
and day and night,
they too are horrible.
And the letter *tā marbouta* is more horrible still,
and at this moment everything the weavers wove
is horrible.
Lord, as I leave the room
I tell You everything is horrible,
yet I feel compelled
to express my thanks as well.

A SPECIAL THANKS

I thank God that these afternoons
which are made of milk
and honey
and ghee
are dripping in the depths of my self.
(As for the invaders, I'll leave them
for another day.)
I thank God
for my share of this afternoon.

A PORTRAIT OF BADIA MASABNI IN CHTOURA [30]

I bought two packs of smokes from her,
and she knew that I knew
who she really was:
Cairo's shining star of the thirties,
the dizzying enchanter
of the men of her era,
the one no world could contain, for no light
was brighter than hers.
She was no Maria Callas
to seclude herself in a Paris apartment
and listen to her old recordings
and die of heartache.
In the movements of her aging body, there was something
of the rhythm of the rumba
and the rustle of Astor Piazzolla's bandoneons,
and it seemed to me that the golden age of the casinos of
    British Egypt
had been abandoned, without much fuss,
on one of the shelves of her shop.

She also seemed to know who I was,
and she may have smiled as she saw me off with a
    vague look,
as I was leaving her shop on that darkening evening,
fifty years ago, on the road to Damascus.

THE FACE OF A FRIEND

For John Berger

A friend's face on the Art History shelf
of a foreign library.
A friend's face from the days of stone houses,
from the days of summer retreats,
from this land that bled you dry so long ago
in a time you no longer remember,
this land that buried you
and raised you from the dead
time and again:
sometimes it buried you
without bringing you back,
sometimes you begged it
to cover you in earth.

What *is* art history, after all,
if not the face of a friend?

A YOUNGER BOY

There's confusion in the evenings, too,
when I think that you
will be a younger girl
in our next life
and that I will be a younger boy
standing beneath the same balcony.

IF YOU ONLY KNEW

For Kamal Boullata[31]

I can't buy my friends from death.
Death buys
but does not sell.

Life said to me:
Buy nothing from death,
it only ever sells itself.
They're yours now, forever.
They're with you now, forever.
If you only knew, your friends
are life itself.

A FORGOTTEN POEM ABOUT FRIENDSHIP

The path bounds joyfully before us
like mountain sheep
in the newborn spring,
while the bells ring
around the sheep's necks.

This is the most a man can do.

A LONG SCAR

You sit in time's haggard furrow,
a furrow devoid of hope, prostrate,
like a long scar on God's eternal face.
You sit while hope crumbles behind you in
    haphazard flames,
while the countries fall, one after the other, behind
    a tyrant,
while the tyrants fall, one after the other, behind
    the countries—
they fall like raindrops on a marsh.

You lie in the slender furrow,
while the earth crumbles behind you,
a long scar on God's eternal face.

A SINGLE SENTENCE

A sentence before the chasms of destruction,
before you fall asleep in the glede's eye,
in the crow's plume,
in the hyena's claw.
A sentence before pus oozes from the horizon,
before the thieves bottle it up
and sell it to tourists,
before one sentence
slays another.
Just one—
a single sentence,
and that's enough.

ENDLESS

In utter darkness,
in light,
in ruin,
in psalms,
in a trumpet,
in the horn of Israfil,
in a labyrinth,
in an end that leads
to an endless end,
I lived.

Translator's Notes

1. Tal al-Samak: This ancient tell or mound, also called Tel Shikmona, is located near Haifa, and has been there since at least antiquity. The verses in italics later in this poem are the opening words of several of the *Mu'allaqat,* perhaps the best-known pre-Islamic Arabic poems (sixth and seventh centuries CE). There are a few words from the poems by Antarah ("Have the poets left anything unsaid?"), Al-Harith ("She announced to us she would soon be parting . . ."), Labid ("The abodes are desolate . . ."), and Abid bin al-Abras ("Emptied of its people . . .").

2. A Verse by Hafez Ibrahim on the Shore of Haifa: "I'm the sea, and the pearls are hidden within me / Did they ask the divers about my shells?" is a verse (composed of two hemistiches) from a well-known poem by the Egyptian poet Hafez Ibrahim (1871–1932) in defense of the Arabic language. The poem is frequently taught in Arab schools.

3. Words for Wadi Salib: Wadi Salib is a neighborhood in Haifa, and the name can be literally translated as "Valley of the Cross."

4. Balad al-Shaykh: The final resting place of Izz al-Din al-Qassam (1881 or 1882–1935), in the district of Haifa. Al-Qassam was a cleric from Syria, and an important anti-colonial figure.

5. A Riding Song with Badawi al-Jabal: Badawi al-Jabal (1903–1981) was a prominent Syrian poet.

6. An Ottoman Tune: The Seferberlik was a forced conscription of Palestinians, Lebanese, Syrians, and Kurds that took place in the waning years of the Ottoman Empire, when the empire was fighting in the Second Balkan War (1913) and then the First World War.

7. Near the Shrine of Saint Naum: This shrine is located in a monastery in North Macedonia. Saint Naum (830–910 CE) was a prominent Bulgarian man of letters, as well as a missionary.

8. Obrigado: "Thank you" in Portuguese.

9. The Poem of Returning Home: Carmel is the name of the mountain that dominates the city of Haifa.

10. On the Way to Tipaza: Tipaza is a coastal city in Algeria.

11. Recalling a Tryst in a Park: "This is the way of lovely women— / they're given to deception": This is from a song by Zakiyya Hamdan (1920–1987), a prominent singer from Aleppo in Syria. The full text of that portion of the song is as follows: "Stand by my grave and say, What part of you was me, and what part of me was you? / I deceived you in life without caring, / and I betrayed you in love, though you never betrayed me. / This is the way of lovely women without protection or rights, / they're given to deception."

12. *Discourses:* These poems, which are called *Mukhatabat* ("discourses") in Arabic, are modeled after a genre of text called *Mukhatabat,* probably the most famous of which were written by the Sufi mystic Al-Niffari (died circa 965 CE). Those texts by Al-Niffari are spiritual discourses of sorts, with each text beginning with the words "He said to me"; the "He" refers to God or the spiritual presence or the higher Self of Al-Niffari himself. Najwan Darwish is playing with that genre here, and diversifying its themes. All of the poems are untitled, and all of them begin with the words "He said to me." The poems are a selection from a much larger group of "Discourses" that Najwan Darwish is writing.

   First Discourse: The Battle of Badr took place in 624 CE in what is now Saudi Arabia. In it, an army led by the Prophet Muhammad (who did not take part in the fighting) decisively defeated an army of non-Muslims from Muhammad's own tribe, the Quraysh, led by Abu Jahl (circa 570–624 CE, also known as Amr ibn Hisham). Abu Jahl, who had been a childhood friend of the Prophet before becoming one of his adversaries, was killed in the fighting.

13. Eighth Discourse: "Every soul shall have a taste of death" is a verse from the Glorious Quran, 3:185.

14. As a Vagabond: "Beauty lived as a vagabond": This is a quotation from Elia Abu Madi (1890–1957), a Lebanese-born poet who later lived in Egypt and the United States.

15. Reading *Uyoun Al-Akhbar* in the Language Academy's Library: The *Uyoun al-Akhbar* ("Book of Choice Narratives") is a multi-volume bi-

ographical history of prominent figures, as well as a compendium of amusing anecdotes, by the renowned Islamic scholar, linguist, and writer Ibn Qutaybah (828–889 CE). The quoted text in this poem is from that work.

16. An Algerian *Nuba:* The Nuba is a melodic form derived from the Andalusian musical tradition, which moved to the countries of the Maghreb and entered into their musical fabric. This poem is composed along the same lines as a well-known Algerian Nuba.

17. Early Riser: The quoted text is by Abdul Jabbar Ibn Hamdis (circa 1056–1133 CE), who was a prominent Sicilian Arab poet who spent part of his life in Al-Andalus, among many other places.

18. I Heard Him Sing: "You, passing by the mills . . ." This line is from a well-known song by the Lebanese singer Fairuz (born 1935).

19. I Remember Umar: Umar ibn al-Khattab (circa 528–644), the second of the four so-called "rightly guided" Caliphs (that is, the direct political successors to the Prophet Muhammad). He was widely known for his just and perspicacious nature. When he captured Jerusalem from the Byzantines in 636–638, he granted the inhabitants of the city their religious freedom, rather than attempting to expel the city's non-Muslim populations.

20. Out of the Depths: "Out of the depths I cry to you, O Lord" is the opening line of Psalm 130.

21. A Conversation with Faris Baroud's Mother in the Al-Shati Camp: Hajja Raya Obaid, better known as Umm Faris (Faris's mother), passed away in the Al-Shati refugee camp in Gaza on May 18, 2017, at the age of eighty-five, after she had completely lost her sight. Her only son, Faris Baroud, was martyred in prison less than two years later, on February 6, 2019, after losing 80 percent of his sight in what was considered deliberate medical negligence following years of physical and psychological torture. Faris Baroud was fifty-one years old when he died, and he spent twenty-eight of those years in various Zionist prisons, including eighteen years in solitary confinement, during which time his family was prevented from visiting him. To this day, the Occupation continues to imprison nearly five thousand Palestinians, including about two hundred children and forty women. (This note is added by the author; the other notes are from the translator.)

22. Take Me, Drag Me Away: Malik Ibn al-Rayb al-Tamimi was a prominent Arab poet from Najd. He is best known for his "self-elegy," a long poem that some historians have said was written as he was awaiting his own death, after having been bitten by a poisonous snake.

23. Mount Carmel: Wadi Nisnas, Wadi Salib, and Kababir are neighborhoods in Haifa.

24. Enough: Darwish dedicated this poem, which was completed in early 2014, to the Danish-Palestinian poet Yahya Hassan (1995–2020). Hassan—who Darwish often described as a younger brother—became a national figure in Denmark when he was only eighteen years old, following the publication of his Danish-language poetry collection YAHYA HASSAN, which sold more than 100,000 copies, a remarkable number for such a small country. Hassan's life was marked by the trauma of the refugee and immigrant experience. He was found dead in his apartment in Aarhus in April 2020, at the age of twenty-four.

25. Boy: The quotations in this poem are from the Sufi mystic Al-Niffari's Book of Stations (which could also be translated as the Book of Stayings or the Book of Standings). This visionary work delves deeply into Al-Niffari's lived experience of the dissolution of the seemingly separate self, which gave way to a kind of unity with God. This poem also contains a reference to a famous expression by the Arab theologian, philosopher, author, and zoologist Al-Jahiz (776–868 or 869 CE): "Meanings are strewn along the road."

26. Tarjiʿ-Band: The title of this poem refers to a genre of poetry from the region of Afghanistan. The muwashah is an Arabic poetic and musical form, and the maqam is a type of Arabic musical melody.

27. Take This Waltz: Sabah Fakhri (1933–2021) was a prominent Syrian singer, and Mohammed Abdel Wahab (1902–1991) was a well-known Egyptian singer and composer.

28. A Variation on a Verse by Al-Maʾarri: Abu Al-Ala Al-Maʾarri (973–1057 CE) was a prominent ascetic Arab poet and philosopher.

29. Little Malta: "Little Malta" was a nickname for Haifa in the seventeenth and eighteenth centuries, when the city briefly rivaled Malta as a haven for pirates and a harbor for stolen ships.

30. A Portrait of Badia Masabni in Chtoura: Badia Masabni (1892–1974) was, among many other things, a prominent Syrian-Lebanese singer, dancer, and performing artist who lived in Egypt for many years, and who has been credited with revolutionizing the art of belly dancing through her famous casino. She later escaped the Egyptian tax authorities and returned to her hometown in Lebanon, where she ran a small shop.

31. If You Only Knew: Kamal Boullata (born in Jerusalem, 1942; died in Berlin, 2019) was a prominent Palestinian artist and art historian.

Credits

Nine poems in this collection ("Mount Carmel," "In Shatila," "Elegy for a Sleeping Child," "Because of a Woman," "A Short Story About the Closing of the Sea," "Exhausted on the Cross," "Enough," "All of It," and "My Defeated Banner") were previously published in *Exhausted on the Cross,* by Najwan Darwish, first published in English by New York Review Books, translation copyright © 2021 by Kareem James Abu-Zeid; reprinted with permission.

Select poems first appeared in the following anthologies or journals:

"Near the Shrine of Saint Naum," originally published in *The Best Literary Translations, 2024* by Deep Vellum, 2024. Also appeared online at *Words Without Borders*/Academy of American Poets, 2022.

"At a Poetry Festival" first appeared online in *Poetry Daily* on November 28, 2023.

"I Often Dream" and "A Variation on a Verse by Al-Ma'arri" first appeared in *Almost Island,* India (Winter 2023 issue).

"Like Everyone Else" and "The Day Leaves You" first appeared in *Poetry's Geographies: A Transatlantic Anthology of Translations* (U.K. edition: Shearsman, 2022; U.S. edition: Eulalia Books, 2023).

"Not This Cup" and "Words for Wadi Salib" first appeared in *Washington Square Review* (Issue 48, Fall 2021).

"Home" and "A Dinner Invitation" first appeared in *Shenandoah* (Spring 2020).

"In Shatila" (also published in *Exhausted on the Cross*) first appeared in *Asymptote* (Winter 2020, 10th Anniversary Issue).

"A Distant Country," "Little Malta," and "A Short Story About the Closing of the Sea" (the latter of which also appeared in *Exhausted on the Cross*) first appeared in *Modern Poetry in Translation,* 2017, Issue 2 (United Kingdom).

"We Never Stop," "If You Only Knew," "Take This Waltz," and "Exhausted on the Cross" (the final of which also appeared in *Exhausted on the Cross*) first appeared in *Cordite Review,* Australia (May 2016).

Mountains crumble in my head first appeared in *Kenyon Review Online* (October 2020).

"An Afternoon in Albaicín" first appeared in *New Poetry in Translation* (Fall 2019 issue).

"I Heard Him Sing" and "You Are Not a Poet in Granada" first appeared in *Two Lines Journal,* Center for the Art of Translation (Spring 2019, 25th Anniversary Issue).

"I Don't Claim" first appeared in *Mizna* ("2019, The Palestine Issue").

"A Verse by Hafez Ibrahim on the Shore of Haifa" first appeared in *The Bellingham Review* (Issue 76, Spring 2018).

"To That Room" (originally called "Rise Again") first appeared in *The Lifted Brow,* Australia (Summer/Fall 2017).

"You Think of a House" (originally called "A Bus Stop in London") first appeared in *This Is Not a Border: Reportage and Reflections from the Palestine Festival of Literature* (Bloomsbury, 2017, United Kingdom).

"No One" first appeared in *Guftugu* magazine, India (Summer 2016).

"Mount Carmel" (originally called "Life in Mount Carmel") first appeared online in *Words Without Borders* (May 2015), and was later published in *Exhausted on the Cross.*

Translator's Acknowledgments

First, I'd like to thank the entire team at the Margellos World Republic of Letters for their extraordinary work on this book. And I'd like to thank Abbie Storch in particular for coming up with the vision for this project and so enthusiastically championing it, and for her skilled editing of the poems and the book as a whole.

I'd also like to thank the many editors—too numerous to name individually here—of journals and magazines who published many of these poems in earlier versions.

I'd like to thank, as always, Najwan Darwish for his warmth and friendship, for his sensitivity and keen eye with the translations, and for placing so much trust in me during the translation process.

I'd also like to thank the two lights of my life, my wife, Paige Cochran, and our little one, Edward, for supporting me in my work, and for always bringing so much joy and laughter into my days.

Finally, I'd like to acknowledge the late poet and translator extraordinaire Jack Hirschman, who introduced me to Najwan so many years ago now. Jack was a man of remarkable creative energy who was responsible for bringing so many different poets and translators together over the years. This book is dedicated to his memory.

NAJWAN DARWISH (born 1978) is one of the foremost contemporary Arab poets. Since the publication of his first collection in 2000, his poetry has been hailed across the Arab world and beyond as a singular expression of the Palestinian struggle. He has published eight books in Arabic, and his work has been translated into more than thirty languages. NYRB Poets published Darwish's *Nothing More to Lose,* translated by Kareem James Abu-Zeid, in 2014, which was selected as one of the best books of the year by NPR and nominated for several awards. His second collection in English, *Exhausted on the Cross,* was published by NYRB Poets in 2021, with a foreword by Raúl Zurita, and was awarded the Sarah Maguire Prize for Poetry in Translation. Darwish lives in Haifa and his birthplace, Jerusalem.

KAREEM JAMES ABU-ZEID (born 1981) is an Egyptian-American translator who translates poetry and fiction from Arabic, French, and German. He has received the Sarah Maguire Prize for Poetry in Translation, a National Endowment for the Arts translation grant, the *Poetry* Magazine Prize for Translation, a Fulbright research fellowship, and PEN Center USA's Translation Prize, among other honors. He has also been a finalist for the PEN America Translation Prize (once in poetry and once in prose), the National Translation Award, the Derek Walcott Prize, and the Banipal Prize for Arabic Translation. He holds a B.A. from Princeton University and a Ph.D. in Comparative Literature from the University of California, Berkeley. His book-length translations include work by Najwan Darwish (Palestine), Adonis (Syria), Dunya Mikhail (Iraq), Rabee Jaber (Lebanon), and Olivia Elias (Palestine). He is also the author of the book *The Poetics of Adonis and Yves Bonnefoy: Poetry as Spiritual Practice,* and he teaches translation workshops around the world.